LLANMADOC AND CHERITON

TWO NORTH GOWER CHURCHES AND THEIR PARISHES

BY

F. G. COWLEY

The Rector and the Llanmadoc and Cheriton
Parochial Church Council
2011

First Published 1993
Second Edition 2011

*All rights reserved.
No part of this book may be reproduced,
stored in a retrieval system or transmitted in any form or by any means,
electronic, mechanical, photocopying, recording or otherwise,
without the written permission of
The Llanmadoc and Cheriton Parochial Church Council*

All profits from this book have been donated to Llanmadoc and Cheriton Churches.
Further copies can be obtained from Llanmadoc and Cheriton PCC,
The Vicarage, Llangennith, Swansea SA3 1HL.

ISBN 978-0-9522046-1-9

Published by The Llanmadoc and Cheriton Parochial Church Council
Copyright © F. G. Cowley

Printed by Dinefwr Press
Llandybie, Carmarthenshire SA18 3YD

CONTENTS

	Page
Foreword by the Bishop of Swansea and Brecon	ii
Foreword by the Rector	iii
The Early Christian Community at Llanmadoc	1
The Anglo-Norman Settlement	
The Church and Manor of Llanmadoc and the Knights Templar	3
The Church of Landimor/Cheriton and the Knights Hospitallers	5
The Medieval Fabric	8
The Reformation	8
Civil War, Commonwealth and Protectorate	10
Llanmadoc and Cheriton in the Eighteenth and Early Nineteenth Centuries	12
The Incumbency of the Revd. J.D. Davies	14
Church Restoration at Llanmadoc and Cheriton	18
The Parsonages:	
Llanmadoc Rectory	21
Glebe House, Cheriton	24
Change, Decay and the Decade of Evangelism	28
Appendices:	
List of Incumbents of Llanmadoc and Cheriton	32
The Church Bells, Church Plate and Stained Glass	34
Fonts and Memorials	35
Sources	37
Acknowledgements	40

Foreword by the Bishop of Swansea and Brecon

It is both a privilege and a pleasure for me to commend to readers the book *'Llanmadoc and Cheriton: Two North Gower Churches and their Parishes'* by Dr. F. G. Cowley. I have read the typescript with great interest. No doubt we were aware already that these two churches were of ancient origin and great historical and architectural interest. Fred Cowley has now given us some fascinating information about the development of each one of them over the centuries.

Today the churches at Llanmadoc and Cheriton are in the care of the Church in Wales. During the hundreds of years of their existence they have experienced many changes in liturgy and worship, as well as in society in general. What splendour there may have been when their walls were most probably covered with paintings - the original visual aids for teaching people the elements of the Christian Faith! Dr. Cowley speculates that the site of the church at Llanmadoc may be exceedingly ancient, just as we know that Christianity came to various parts of Britain, including Wales, in primitive times. Gower today still reflects certain aspects of its Anglo-Norman past, but behind that there is an even longer Christian tradition.

Some of the incumbents of these churches held office for many years. But none did so for a longer period, or made a greater impression than the Revd. J.D. Davies. We are united with them in the great Communion of Saints and in bearing witness to the Faith, which they held dear, and is still alive in those who acknowledge themselves to be disciples of Jesus Christ in this 20th Century. I hope that the efforts to restore the church at Cheriton and cherish that at Llanmadoc will achieve great success. I hope, too, that Dr. Cowley's book will be accorded the credit it deserves.

+Dewi Swansea and Brecon

Foreword by The Rector

The Church in Wales is facing a great dilemma as far as its stock of churches is concerned. Due to the mobility of the population during the past century there are places with too many church buildings and the converse is also true. Some would plead for the traditional easy accessibility of a place to worship God. On the other hand, there is a clarion call to rationalise the situation by declaring redundant those churches that are rarely used or have very small congregations. If the latter position were adopted in this Parish, a strong case could be made for closing one of the churches. The reality is that they are only one mile apart and St. Madoc, located as it is in the Village, would be the logical one to remain open.

Bearing in mind the current debate, which seems to ignore the spiritual heritage of ancient seats of Christian worship. I am of the opinion that the members of Llanmadoc and Cheriton Parochial Church Council have taken courageous and farsighted decisions. After a great deal of discussion and soul searching they resolved to restore both the Church of St. Madoc in Llanmadoc and St. Cadoc in Cheriton.

Decisions were followed by actions. A quinquennial inspection carried out on St. Cadoc in autumn 1991 confirmed the fears of the PCC that there would be need for an extensive programme of restoration. Mr. Martin Glass was appointed Architect and he engaged Abbey Masonry to undertake the work. The process took a couple of years and in the intervening time St. Madoc has had minor but necessary attention paid to it so that it is a pleasant place to offer prayer, praise and thanksgiving to the Lord our God.

I am confident that when the restoration project has been completed on Cheriton Church it will be seen as the product of good stewardship. The heritage that has been placed into our care will be handed on in the knowledge that the building is still an architectural gem and an integral part of the history and landscape of Gower.

This history of the Church in Llanmadoc and Cheriton, which has been so knowledgeably written by Dr. Cowley, will help to enhance the information already in print about the Parishes and of its most famous Rector, John D. Davies. As it is right to retell the long and honourable spiritual heritage of this area of North Gower, so it is important to build up an archive of its history during this Century. Therefore, information, whether anecdotal or written regarding the life of the people and their clerics would be most valuable for a future publication.

Llanmadoc Church from the west

Cheriton Church from the south

The Early Christian Community at Llanmadoc

Llanmadoc is the smallest church in Gower and with an area of 1,514 acres its parish is also among the smaller of the Gower parishes. Yet the church possesses in the nave evidence for being the site of one of the earliest Christian communities in the peninsula. In 1861 the Revd. J.D. Davies, the rector of Llanmadoc, found embedded in the wall of his rectory, the incomplete remains of an early-inscribed Christian memorial stone. He removed it and had it set with an explanatory brass plaque into the windowsill of the south wall of the church nave where it still remains. The Latin inscription is in two lines and the surviving text of the Advectus stone reads:

VECTI FILIUS
GVANI HIC IACIT

which translated reads:

OF...VECTUS SON
OF GVANUS HE LIES HERE

The Latin formula used - Hic iacit - and the style of Roman capitals indicate that this is a memorial grave-marker to a Christian who died in the late fifth or early sixth century (475 A.D. to 525 A.D.). The lettering is very obviously technically inferior to the regularly spaced and symmetrical lettering found on inscriptions in the main urban and military centres of Roman Britain, at Caerleon for example. The Latin grammar is also corrupt. The *Hic iacit* should read *Hic iacet*. However, a memorial of even this debased kind would not have been erected to a nonentity. Vectus or Advectus (if there are missing letters) must have been a man of some importance in his local community, and one can therefore infer that a small Christian community existed in northwest Gower at this early period.

One can perhaps even go a little farther. Archaeologists now tell us that many early Christian churches had their origins in small enclosed cemeteries. Such cemeteries having a grave-marker to an important churchman or layman as a focus for future burials, would be used by Christians as meeting places for worship, and particularly for the celebration of the Eucharist, before churches were built. Llanmadoc may have developed in this way. First the burial of a prominent churchman or layman forming the nucleus for further burials, then the erection of a wooden oratory, later to be replaced by a stone-built church. Llanmadoc is certainly the earliest Christian site in Gower for which we have unimpeachable evidence.

By the time the Advectus stone had been erected the Christian church had already been in existence in Britain for some centuries. Christianity had reached Britain by 200 A.D. give or take a decade or so. By about 300 A.D. Christian bishops had established their sees in important Roman towns and were soon to be attending major church councils on the continent. By this time the bishops, assisted by their priests and deacons, had already begun the work of conversion within Britain. However, the process was halted in lowland Britain after 450 A.D. by the settlement of the pagan Anglo-Saxons. It is even possible that the organization of the church was destroyed in this area until the arrival of Augustine in 597 A.D. when the work of evangelization was resumed. In the west, however, in what is now Wales, Cornwall and Devon, the church survived, though its organization may have had to be modified to suit changed circumstances. Gildas, a Christian cleric, who wrote about 548 A.D., was a Jeremiah lamenting the ills of his own time. He has little good to say of society or of the surviving church in Wales at this period but even he was able to detect signs of hope. He speaks of "a few, a very few...the only true sons...the holy mother the Church has left. By their prayers they support my weakness from total collapse, like posts and columns of salvation." Gildas was almost certainly referring to the monks who were establishing their monasteries in western Britain in the late fifth and early sixth centuries.

Christian monasticism had its origins in the arid deserts of Egypt and Syria at the end of the third century. Stories of the spiritual exploits of "desert fathers" like St. Anthony and St. Basil were taken back to the west by Christian tourists and pilgrims and by the fifth century monasteries of similar type were being established in Gaul, western Britain and Ireland. In Glamorgan the most famous of these monasteries were at Llantwit Major (Llanilltud Fawr), founded by Illtud about the year 500 A.D. and at Llancarfan, founded by Cadoc not long afterwards. We know from an historical miscellany known as *Historia Brittonum,* and attributed to Nennius (fl.800 A.D.), that Illtud soujourned in Gower for a time either at Oystermouth or Oxwich. The churches of Oxwich, Ilston and Llanrhidian are all dedicated to him. This does not mean that he founded these churches but it is possible that he or his disciples may have undertaken missionary work or held monastic estates in Gower in the sixth century. The evidence of the Llanmadoc stone needs to be seen against this background of renewed activity in the British church when Gildas was writing his jeremiad.

There are two other early Christian stones in Llanmadoc church that suggest that the church became an important ecclesiastical centre in the period between 600 A.D. and 1100 A.D. One is a pillar stone with an inscribed cross on the widest part of its face. It was found in the churchyard in 1864 and its design indicates that it was probably erected at some time between the seventh and ninth centuries (650 AD. to 850 A.D.) It now occupies a recess in the west end of the nave. The other is a broken pillar stone of about the same date with two inscribed crosses. It too was found in the churchyard in 1864 and now occupies a recess in the west wall of the nave. The compilers of the Royal Commission Inventory of the early Christian monuments of Glamorgan have stated "the three early monuments at Llanmadoc...together with its coastal situation and the survival of a hand bell of Celtic type, suggest that something more than merely a local church was established here". Jeremy Knight, former Inspector of Ancient Monuments for CADW has conjectured that Llanmadoc may have been an important minster church with sub-churches and property spread over west Gower.

The so-called Celtic bell was ploughed up in a field called Parc-yr-Odyn (Field of the Kiln) near Cwm Ivy. It came into the possession of C.R.M. Talbot and was placed in his museum at Penrice and was subsequently donated to the National Museum of Wales by his daughter Emily. When the Revd. J.D. Davies first recorded it, it was hopefully thought it might have been an ecclesiastical hand bell of the type which was so highly prized in Celtic lands in medieval times. Used to call the faithful to prayer it could acquire the status of a powerful relic if it had been repeatedly used by a man of acknowledged sanctity. However, in 1979 the then-Keeper of Archaeology at the National Museum of Wales, Mr. J. M. Lewis, re-examined the Llanmadoc bell and compared it with other examples at St. Fagans Folk Museum. He came to the conclusion that the Llanmadoc bell was a cow bell, probably of seventeenth century date.

The fact that the saint's name Madoc is enshrined in the place-name Llanmadoc and that this place-name is mentioned as early as 1156 is good evidence that the church was dedicated to Madoc before the Anglo-Norman settlement of Gower. Who the Madoc of Llanmadoc was is a question difficult to answer with any certainty. Madoc or Maidoc is an affectionate Irish nickname for Aidan and the Llanmadoc Madoc has been identified with an Irish Aidan, monk and bishop who was born in Connaught, founded the monasteries of Ferns, Drumlane and Rossinver and is accredited with incredible feats of austerity, such as fasting on barley bread and water for seven years, as well as reciting 500 psalms daily. He occurs in Rhigyfarch's *Life of St. David* and Lifris's *Life of St. Cadog*, as well as having an Irish life devoted to him. Writers of saints' lives, however, were notorious plagiarists and lives of saints of similar name have become inextricably confused. The dates given for the feast day of Madoc add to the confusion. William of Worcester gives his feast day as 31st January as does his Irish Life. A medieval calendar of saints composed at Monmouth priory gives it as 28th February. Yet the patronal festival at Llanmadoc was always kept on 12th November. The true identity of Madoc is likely to remain elusive. We know virtually nothing of Llanmadoc before the Norman Conquest. Its coastal position may have made it vulnerable to Viking raids which we know were frequent along the Welsh coast during the tenth century and the existence of Scandinavian place-names and stray finds of Norse jewellery in west Gower make this likely. But there was no shortage of native despoilers at this period. Gower was ravaged by Welsh princes in 970, 977 and 991.

The Anglo-Norman Settlement of Gower

The Church and Manor of Llanmadoc and the Knights Templar

At the beginning of the twelfth century the mist that beclouds the early history of Llanmadoc begins to clear a little. In 1106 the last native prince to hold the commote of Gower, Hywel ap Goronwy, was strangled and beheaded by the Normans and the commote was acquired by the Norman lord Henry, earl of Warwick. He built his main castle at Swansea and then began distributing the richer and more fertile lands of the peninsula to his followers and also to a favoured abbey in Normandy. Between 1106 and 1119 Henry earl of Warwick granted the churches and lands which once belonged to an early monastery or minster at Llangennith to the Norman abbey of St. Taurin, Evreux, and Llangennith became a small dependent Benedictine cell containing a prior and a companion monk. In 1156 Henry's wife Margaret, countess of Warwick (who probably held Gower by right of dower after the death of her husband) granted the vill and church of Llanmadoc to the military order of the Knights Templar. This was an order of warrior-monks founded in 1119 by the French knight Hugh de Payns, to police the roads and protect the pilgrim routes in the newly established Latin kingdom and its satellite principalities. These came into being in the Holy Land as a result of the first Crusade (1095-99). Donations of land and churches flowed in and made necessary some form of organisation to exploit the order's resources. In England the headquarters of the order was at the Temple Church in the Strand, London. But in the provinces the property of the order was administered from regional preceptories. The Templar property at Llanmadoc with other property in South Wales at Narbeth and Pembroke was administered from the preceptory of Garway in Herefordshire.

The grant of the church at Llanmadoc needs explanation. What was conveyed was not the income of the church, derived from the glebe, tithes and offerings, but the 'advowson' or right of presentation to the living. The living remained a rectory and the rector was presented to the church by the preceptor of Garway and instituted by the bishop of St. David's. The manor of Llanmadoc in terms of cultivatable acreage was quite small, about 115 acres, and would not have justified the residence of an officer of the order. It was probably exploited by a local reeve responsible to an officer from Garway who would pay periodic visits to Llanmadoc to collect its revenues.

Apart from the military service they rendered in the Holy Land the Knights Templar became international bankers, providing places of secure deposit for money and valuables, financing loans and operating a sort of Securicor service to guard money in transit. The failure of the thirteenth century crusades and the fall of Acre to the Muslims in 1291 robbed the order of its chief *raison d'être*. Criticism of the order mounted and was orchestrated by the French king, Philip IV, who saw the confiscation of the vast wealth of the Templars as a means of replenishing his depleted treasury. Philip IV moved against the order in 1307 and ordered the arrest of its officers. They were then subjected to torture to elicit from them false confessions of heresy, sexual perversion and ritual murder. The English king followed suit. Secret orders were issued by the king on 20th December 1307 to arrest all Knights of the Temple on 7th January 1308. The royal sheriff of Carmarthen, accompanied by an escort of twelve horsemen, rode over to Llanmadoc to take possession of the Templar manor there. A statement of accounts still exists in the Public Record Office, London, which gives a detailed report on the issues of the manor between 8th January and 29th September 1308.

As has been said, the manor was quite small and the report accounted for little more than 115 acres. Sixty acres of these were held and worked by husbandmen and fifty two acres were demesne land worked exclusively for the profit of the Templars. The account mentions 11 husbandmen, 4 cottars and 4 men in advowry, which gives some idea of the small scale of agricultural operations here.

In 1312 Pope Clement V formally suppressed the order of Knights Templar and ordered that its property should be transferred to the Knights Hospitallers. The Templar property at Llanmadoc with the other property of the Order in South Wales, fell within the bailiwick of the Templar preceptory of Garway in Herefordshire. The whole of this bailiwick was now transferred to the care of the Hospitaller preceptory of Dinmore, also in Herefordshire.

The Church of Landimor/Cheriton and the Knights Hospitaller

Immediately to the east of the parish and manor of Llanmadoc lay the fee or manor of Landimor, an extensive holding extending in one or maybe two parts from the Burry stream to Cil Ifor, with a further detached part at Rhosili. It had been acquired by the Turbervill family as part of the Anglo-Norman settlement of Gower in the early twelfth century. Sometime before 1165 William Turbervill granted "the church of Llanridian, with its chapel of Walterston (*capella villae Walteri*), the church of 'Llandunnor' and the church of Rossilly" (all churches within the fee of Landimor) to the Knights Hospitallers of St. John of Jerusalem. Like the Knights Templar, this military order had its origins in the Holy Land and aimed to provide military protection and hospital care to Christian pilgrims to Jerusalem. During the twelfth century it acquired extensive property throughout Europe. Its headquarters in England and Wales was at St. John's Clerkenwell, London, but in the provinces its property was exploited from commanderies or preceptories. In St. David's diocese the order's property was administered from the commandery of Slebech in Pembrokeshire.

All authorities are agreed that 'Llandunnor' is a misspelling or misreading of Landimor. This is a reasonable assumption since the text of the charter in which William Turbervill's grant is recorded, has only survived in a late transcript. Nevertheless there is still a good deal of uncertainty and controversy about the age and location of the church of Landimor mentioned in the charter. The Revd. J.D. Davies, the celebrated antiquary and former rector of Llanmadoc and Cheriton, argued that a church in or near the village of Landimor was the original church which served Cheriton parish, that it was abandoned in the late thirteenth century probably because of the encroachment of the sea, and that the present church of Cheriton was built to replace it. He used a number of arguments to support his claim. After its mention in the charter, it is next mentioned as Landimor in the valuation of church property known as the *Taxation of Pope Nicholas* dated 1291. The place-name Cheriton first occurs in a deed dated about the years 1330-40. The church is subsequently mentioned as the church of Cheryton in the valuation known as the *Valor Ecclesiasticus* dated 1535. Davies reasonably assumed from the change of name that the church had changed its site. He considered that two other pieces of evidence strengthened his case. The Welsh place-name Landimor could be interpreted to mean 'church by or of the sea' and many churches were indeed lost to the sea in the inundations recorded in the late thirteenth and early fourteenth centuries. Again, the *Mapsant,* the patronal festival of the saint to whom the church was dedicated, was held at Landimor village, not at Cheriton, "of itself", wrote Davies, "a sufficient proof that a church once existed in or near the village of Landimor. The existence of a mapsant invariably implies the existence of a church".

Despite these weighty arguments in favour of a change of site, there are also telling arguments against Davies's theory. The surviving episcopal registers of St. David's were not readily available to Davies. They were not published until 1917, six years after his death. In them the church is referred to as Landimor in documents as late as 1513 and 1517, two centuries or so after we know Cheriton church existed. When a church is abandoned it usually leaves some record in folk memory, in a field name or even in physical remains. The assumed church has left no such remains. One abandoned church in north Gower has left remains - the walls of the medieval chapel of St. Michael, Cwrtycarnau near Pontardulais can still be traced in the mud flats. Davies was himself puzzled by this: "not a trace of it is now to be found, and strange to say, there is not even a tradition among the people of the existence of any such building".

The place-name Landimor need not necessarily mean 'church by or of the sea'. The second element may be a personal name and the prefix 'Lan' may not be church but a corruption of another word. Two further arguments deserve consideration. The core of the glebe land, the land anciently set aside for the support of a priest at the church's consecration, is shown in the tithe map of 1846 as lying around the church at Cheriton with only two fragments of pasture, just an acre in extent, on the salt marsh below Landimor village. Lastly, if the church had been in or near Landimor and had been abandoned, would the villagers of Landimor have consented to its replacement being built at the opposite end of the parish?

According to this view then, Landimor and Cheriton are one and the same church. But why was it built where it is, less than a mile from Llanmadoc church? It is possible that the church was constructed in the early to mid-twelfth century to serve the needs of the residents of the primitive ringwork castle at North Hill Tor which lay less than half a mile to the north of the church. The earthwork at North Hill Tor is marked as an "earthwork" on the Ordnance Survey map but the Royal Commission on Ancient Monuments for Wales have, in their recently published volume *Glamorgan: the Early Castles from the Norman Conquest to 1217* identified it as a twelfth century ringwork castle. The pattern of a primitive castle with a newly- constructed church nearby is a marked feature of Anglo-Norman settlement in south Wales and Gower examples can be seen at Penrice where the motte castle (Mountybank) lies just west of the church and at Penmaen where the church lies (now in ruins) to the north of the ringwork on the cliff edge. (It has recently come to light that the field immediately above the Church is described on the 1845 Tithe Maps as Castlage, which may well be significant)

If this view is accepted, Cheriton, despite its dedication to the sixth century saint Cadoc, is not an ancient church like Llanmadoc - significantly no early Christian stone has been found at Cheriton nor indeed in any other part of the parish. The church was probably built, and its parish carved out of the large sprawling parish of Llanrhidian, sometime in the early twelfth century. Llanrhidian, it needs to be said, is an ancient church, like Llanmadoc, and has claims to be considered an early centre of Christianity in Gower dating from the sixth century.

Parochial boundaries were important when a parson derived a major part of his income from tithe. He needed to know from whom he could legally claim tithe and this made necessary a careful demarcation of parochial boundaries. Fortunately a detailed description of the bounds of the parish of Cheriton has survived. They were copied by Revd. J.D. Davies from a written copy dated 1747 and deserve to be quoted:

It is headed thus:- "An account of the boundaries of the Parish of Cheriton dividing from the adjoining Parishes.

"Beginning at the low water mark on Llandimore sands with strait course from thence to the ditch that divides between Townsend farm and Wibley Castle farm. a strait hedge from thence to the road that leads from Landymore to Llanrhidian crossing the road taking the strait hedge through the Windmill farm to the road that leads from Mansel's fould to Burry river, then taking the hedge that borders that road at the North and West sides down to the river, then by the river's side down to the hedge that leads to Rhyers Down between Thos.Mansel Talbot's land and Chas. Edwin Esq., then crossing the mountain to Green Wells corner, from thence across the mountain to the south side of the horse pit to crow well by the stream to the bottom of the mountain turning then to the right hand and taking the hedge that decides between great rurough and little rurough strait to Llanmadock hill turning to the left up the bulwarks corner from thence down to Dervins wells following the stream of water to the river burry and from thence to the low water mark at Whitford."

"A copy of the boundaries of the parish of Cheriton. Thus drafted in the year 1747 by us whose names are hereunto subscribed.

>*HENRY LUCAS, Esq. Townsend*
>*JOSEPH WALKER, Bovehill*
>*DAVID SMITH, Northill*
>*THOMAS LEWIS, Landymore*
>*WM. EVANS, Stembridge"*

Revd. J.D. Davies found another copy of the bounds among his father's papers, which added after bringing the boundary down to low water mark at Whitford – *"from thence across the salt sand to take Lanstofen Steepel."*

Whether the original church serving the parish was at Landimor or Cheriton, the present church is a re-build. We have no means of determining what the original church looked like, of what materials it was made, whether of wood or stone. Unlike most Gower churches, however, which are examples of folk-building rather than fine architecture, the present church at Cheriton has a distinctive, recognizable architectural style and has claims to be regarded as the finest church in Gower. It is built in the Early English style and consists of nave, a choir surmounted by a tower with saddleback roof and a chancel. The hall-marks of the Early English style can best be seen inside: the ornately carved inner doorway from the porch to the nave with its foliage mouldings, the pointed arches supporting the tower which terminate at their bases with beautifully carved corbels and the narrow lancet windows in the south walls of the nave, tower and chancel.

Although the features of the Early English style are clear enough at Cheriton, the building is difficult to date with precision. It is difficult to know how long it took new fashions in architecture to pass from the areas of good building stone, where they usually originated, to areas like Gower, which in medieval times were poor and remote. So it is not surprising that the experts have offered varying opinions on the date of the fabric at Cheriton.

Laurence Butler, writing in the *Glamorgan County History* says of Cheriton that "the prevailing impression is that the church was newly-constructed in the first decades of the thirteenth century." Elizabeth Beazley and Peter Howell give it a mid-thirteenth century date in the *Collins Guide to the Parish Churches of England and Wales* and R. W. Soden in his *Guide to Welsh Parish Churches* calls Cheriton "a beautiful late-thirteenth century church" The Revd. J.D. Davies whose opinion deserves respect - he was an ecclesiologist keenly interested in church architecture - suggested that the church might be fourteenth century and "if so would correspond with the conventual buildings called the glebe house... supposed to be fourteenth century. ' It is indeed highly probable that Cheriton Church and its parsonage, Glebe House were built more or less contemporaneously. But if Davies is right it suggests an even more intriguing thought. Was the church and parsonage built out of the proceeds of the confiscated Templar estates, which fell to the Hospitallers after 1312? Something more will be said about Glebe House on a later page.

Fortunately for the Hospitallers their order did not come under the criticism, attack and confiscation suffered by the Templars, and the Commandery of Slebech continued to hold the patronage of Cheriton church down to 1540 when the order was dissolved.

The Medieval Fabric

Although the churches of Llanmadoc and Cheriton had assumed the structural form we can still see today, before the year 1350 both churches would have presented, within and without, a very different appearance in medieval times. The exterior walls would have been white or colour washed, as was the north Gower church of Llandeilo Talybont before its demolition in the 1980s. The nave and chancel would have been roofed not with Caernarvonshire slate, which from the early nineteenth century has been the usual roof covering for Gower churches, but with grey Welsh flags. Some Gower churches were even thatched. The interior walls would also have been plastered, and covered with paintings illustrating incidents and episodes from the Old and New Testaments and from the lives of the saints. When the churches of Llanmadoc and Cheriton were restored in 1865 and 1875 respectively, the Revd. J.D. Davies noticed fragments of design and texts adhering to parts of the hacked down plaster and recorded what he could of what was visible. But there was no time for a careful examination. It may be that religious paintings of high quality adorned the walls of these churches, of a kind which have been preserved and restored at the Welsh National History Museum from the now defunct church at Llandeilo Talybont.

A major feature of interior furnishing which a medieval worshipper could not help noticing was the rood beam and screen. The rood beam lay across the chancel arch, rested on corbels and supporting a platform on which was fixed an image of Christ crucified, flanked by images of the Blessed Virgin and St. John. The platform would often be decorated with flowers and illuminated with candles. The doorway, which gave access to the rood loft, can still be seen to the left of the chancel arch at Llanmadoc and a similar doorway survives at Cheriton.

The wooden screen below the rood beam effectively separated the congregation from the clergy in the eastern part of the church and the priest celebrated Mass on a stone altar in the chancel area with his back to the people.

The Reformation

In 1534 Master John Davy, rector of Llanmadoc and Porteynon, and other clerics in the deanery of Gower, put their signatures to the statement that "the Bishop of Rome has not any greater jurisdiction in this kingdom of England than any other foreign bishop" There is no signature for the incumbent of Cheriton. The rector may have been a non-resident pluralist who held a living or livings in another deanery and signed the declaration there. In the next few years a series of acts of Parliament inspired by Henry VIII and his minister Thomas Cromwell put an end to the pope's jurisdiction in England and Wales and substituted in its place the Royal supremacy. The following half century witnessed a radical transformation of the interiors of most of the churches of England and Wales. The religious paintings, which had provided visual aids to enable the illiterate to understand the Christian message, were covered with lavish coats of whitewash and scriptural texts and the royal coat of arms painted in their place. The stone altars were taken out and replaced with wooden tables. The stone altar at Cheriton was even used as part of the step into the chancel. Carved images of the saints and holy water stoups were also removed. A vernacular liturgy of great literary beauty enshrined in the Book of Common Prayer replaced the Latin Mass.

How the clergy and people of Gower reacted to these momentous changes cannot really be determined because so few of them had the means or ability to convey their feelings and thoughts to posterity. But slowly, perhaps more slowly in remote areas like Gower, the interior appearance of parish churches was changed.

Cheriton church c. 1850

Civil War, Commonwealth and Protectorate (1642/1660)

The tensions inherent in the Elizabethan church settlement - the tug between those who wished to retain a Catholic ethos in the liturgy and ornaments of the church and those who wished for more radical Protestant change at all levels - were never really resolved and played a major part in the conflict between king and parliament which eventually resulted in the outbreak of the Civil War (1642-49) and the establishment of the republican Commonwealth (1649-53) and Protectorate (1653-60). This period was one of anxiety, bitterness and real hardship for the clergy and parishioners of Gower parishes as elsewhere.

In 1643 the Long Parliament abolished episcopacy and endeavoured to ensure that altars, crosses, statues and candlesticks, which remained in churches, were removed. Two years later Archbishop Laud was executed, the Book of Common Prayer was abolished and a Puritan-inspired service book, the Directory, set in its place. But the real upheaval for many clergy and their parishioners came with the passing in 1650 of the Act for the Propagation of the Gospel in Wales. This was a deliberate attempt to puritanize Wales. Commissioners were appointed to examine incumbents and eject those guilty of delinquency and malignancy (that is to say, clinging to Anglican practices) and non-residence. Eight Gower incumbents were ejected from their livings, among them George Parry, rector of Llanmadoc and Cheriton. He was succeeded at Llanmadoc by Morgan Jones who had been intruded by the commissioners. John Walker, the Anglican chronicler of this period, calls him "an ignorant fellow, one Jones" but Edward Calamy, a partisan of the puritan cause, was kinder and preferred to refer to him as "an honest ploughman" At Cheriton the Baptist Thomas Proud was intruded.

Soon after the restoration of Charles II in 1662, an Act of Uniformity was passed which required all church ministers to accept a newly revised Prayer Book. Morgan Jones and Thomas Proud were now ejected and the livings of Llanmadoc and Cheriton restored to George Parry. George Parry composed a metrical version of the psalms in Welsh and has the distinction, shared with Revd. J.D. Davies, of being the only rectors of Llanmadoc and Cheriton, to have articles devoted to them in the *Dictionary of Welsh Biography*. Parry died in 1678 and was buried in an unmarked grave in Cheriton churchyard.

Llanmadoc church chancel c. 1850

Llanmadoc and Cheriton in the Eighteenth and early Nineteenth Centuries

The Church in this period has had a poor press. Contemporary satirical cartoonists as well as historians have characterized it as a Church debilitated by torpor, complacency and neglect. It is indeed true that the clergy after the bitter sectarian conflicts of the seventeenth century wanted peace and stability, untroubled by extremism or 'enthusiasm'. But the more the period has been studied in recent years, both at parochial and diocesan level, the more some of the more damning generalizations have had to be modified. At the outset it needs to be remembered that Welsh livings were extremely poor. At the beginning of the eighteenth century Llanmadoc was only worth £38 per annum and Cheriton £39. A clergyman with a growing family to support would seek to augment the meagre income from one living by acquiring additional ones or at least a curacy in an adjoining parish. This meant non-residence at additionally acquired livings and the employment of curates. Thus in 1755 the Revd. Richard Price, rector of Llanmadoc who does not appear to have held another living in the deanery of Gower, employed a curate, William Jenkins, to serve his living. In 1804 Llanmadoc was still being served by a curate, the Revd. James Edwards, and his rector, the Revd. Samuel Davies resided in Shalford in Surrey. However, James Edwards was not a penniless curate - he held the rectory of Reynoldston as well as his curacy. In 1821 he himself became rector of Llanmadoc. The situation was much the same at Cheriton. It was served in 1799 by a curate, Revd. R. Jones, at a stipend of £15 per annum for the rector, Benjamin Jones, who was non-resident. Arrangements of this kind of course pre-dated the eighteenth century and may well have been common practice in medieval times.

What of the level of pastoral care enjoyed by the two parishes in the same period? Until the Revd. J.D. Davies became rector of Llanmadoc and curate of Cheriton in 1860, the frequency of services had remained stable for a considerable period. Each church had one service each Sunday, which alternated between a morning service at 10 a.m. and an afternoon service at 2p.m. in the winter and somewhat later in the summer. At Llanmadoc Holy Communion was celebrated four times a year: at Easter, Whitsun, Michaelmas and Christmas with 20-25 communicants, while at Cheriton, Holy Communion was celebrated every six weeks with about the same number of communicants as Llanmadoc. Children were catechised on Sundays in Lent.

The churchwardens and parishioners of Llanmadoc responded enthusiastically to the circulating schools initiated by Griffith Jones, rector of Llanddowror. His aim was to promote a level of literacy in the parishes of Wales, which would enable parishioners to read the Bible and Prayer Book. This was to be achieved by sending around on circuit qualified teachers to hold schools in the winter months when adults and children could attend. Schools were held at Llanmadoc in the winter months of 1764-5, 1765-6 and 1766-67 and 71, 44 and 39 pupils respectively attended. In the parishes of West Gower the schools were conducted in English. They were remarkably successful. The Revd. R. Jones, curate of Cheriton, reported in the visitation returns of 1804 that his poor parishioners could read and write English but they were not furnished with any books when they came to church. Hymn singing was suspect at this time and considered best left to the Methodists and dissenters. As the curate of Cheriton was careful to point out in 1804 nothing was sung in the church "but the words of scripture". The services at this time were led by the curate with the responses from the parish clerk and the more literate farmers.

The rectorships of Rev. Prosser Pearce at Llanmadoc (1835-60) and Revd. William Lucas Collins at Cheriton (1815-67) were a transitional period for both parishes. The Church in rural areas like Gower was slowly being made aware of a new tide of reform, for by the 1830s the Church at national level and with government initiative was beginning to put its house in order. The Ecclesiastical Commission was set up in 1835 and a series of acts of Parliament passed - the Tithe Commutation Act (1836), the Pluralities Act (1836), the Established Church Act (1836) and the Ecclesiastical Duties and Revenues Act (1840) - which aimed at making a more equitable distribution of the Church's income, removing long-standing abuses and providing the Church with a more efficient machinery for discharging its functions. The effects of these measures were not felt immediately. The Revd. Prosser Pearce, unlike many of his eighteenth century predecessors, resided at Llanmadoc and occupied the rather ramshackle old rectory (the predecessor of the present 'rectory' which is now in private hands) opposite the church until his death. William Lucas Collins, rector of Cheriton, however, was non-resident and obtained a succession of episcopal licences to reside elsewhere on the grounds that the parsonage house - Glebe House - was unfit for habitation. This was partly a fiction, as we shall see below. About 1853 Collins and his family moved to Northamptonshire where he had acquired a number of curacies. He continued to hold these with Cheriton until 1867 when he was appointed rector of Kilsby (1867-73). In 1873 he was appointed rector of Lowick with the vicarage of Slipton in 1876. He forfeited Cheriton in 1867 and resided on his Lowick living until his death. He was also an honorary canon of Peterborough Cathedral.

William Lucas Collins is the only rector of Cheriton to have found a place in the *Dictionary of National Biography*. He was a churchman of the 'high and dry school', a keen cricketer and a fine scholar. He edited the series 'Ancient Classics for English Readers' to which he himself contributed ten volumes. His other works include *The Luck of Ladysmede* (1860), *The Education Question* (1862) and *Etonians Ancient and Modern* (1865).

Collins was an intimate friend of Anthony Trollope whose Barchester novels provided such an entertaining commentary on the Church of England during the age of reform. He lent Trollope Lowick Rectory to enable him to write his novel *Dr. Wortle's School*. "That I, who have belittled so many clergyman", wrote Trollope to Collins, "should ever come to live in a parsonage! You may be sure that I will endeavour to behave myself accordingly, so that no scandal shall fall upon the parish...Ought I to affect dark garments? Say the word and I will supply myself with a high waistcoat. Will it be right to be quite genial with the curate? If there be dissenters, should I frown on them, or smile blandly? If a tithe pig be brought, shall I eat him? If they take to address me as "The Rural Anthony", will it be alright?"

The Incumbency of Revd. John David Davies (1860-1911)

The appointment of Revd. J.D. Davies as curate of Cheriton in 1860, as rector of Llanmadoc in the same year, and as rector of the consolidated livings of Llanmadoc and Cheriton in 1868, marks an important landmark in the ecclesiastical history of Gower and indeed of the diocese of St. David's. He was the first priest to introduce the principles of the Oxford Movement into the old deanery of Gower. This movement was started in 1833 by a group of Oxford dons who were concerned for the security of the Church in a period when established institutions were coming under criticism and attack. Newman, Keble and Pusey viewed the Church as a divine society whose ministers derived their authority not from the state but by direct descent from the apostles themselves by the laying on of hands. They were dispensers of divinely instituted sacraments, which were regarded as the chief means of conveying grace and as guarantees of personal holiness and salvation. The thrust of the movement was to emphasize the Catholic element in the Church of England. Between 1833 and 1841 ninety tracts were issued which propounded the principles of the movement giving its supporters the name 'Tractarians'. By the time Davies was ordained priest the movement had expanded to embrace new ideas and practices - the introduction of a richer ceremonial into church services and of new furniture to provide fitting accompaniments for the church's sacramental life: choir stalls, sedilia, credence tables and altar frontals. Some of the movement's supporters were now calling themselves Anglo-Catholics. Davies was the first priest in Gower, perhaps in the diocese of St. David's, to wear the Eucharistic vestments since the Reformation changes of the sixteenth century, having introduced them at Llanmadoc and Cheriton in 1865. He also instituted a surpliced choir and since he was a gifted musician, acted as his own choirmaster. He himself adopted the clerical dress of an Anglo-Catholic priest: the multi-buttoned cassock with sash and the Roman biretta.

Davies was born in Gower, the son of the rector of Reynoldston but it is difficult to trace the varying strands of influence which went to form his particular brand of churchmanship. The deanery of Gower, or rather the two deaneries into which it had become divided in the nineteenth century, was an area of 'low' evangelical style churchmanship. Neither Rossall School, Lancashire, nor Trinity College Dublin, where he received his education, were centres of high church or Anglo-Catholic influence. But Davies was a member of the Ecclesiological Society (the former Cambridge Camden Society) and received *The Ecclesiologist*, a periodical that advocated traditional Catholic modes of worship in the Church of England. He would not have been able to transform his two livings into a stronghold of Anglo-Catholicism, however, without the support of the Talbot family of Margam and Penrice and of Starling Benson of Fairy Hill. C.R.M. Talbot was a substantial landowner in Llanmadoc and Cheriton parishes and his children were committed Anglo-Catholics. When they were at their London town-house in Cavendish Square they attended All Saints, Margaret Street, the fashionable cathedral of Anglo-Catholicism in London. Starling Benson helped to finance the building of the new church school on Llanmadoc Hill, which operated between 1870 and 1935. His half-brother, Richard Meux Benson, was an Anglo-Catholic priest and founded the religious order known as the Cowley Fathers. With powerful support of this kind behind him, Davies was able to introduce all the accompaniments of Anglo-Catholic worship and to weather any storm of criticism, whether it came from within or outside his parishes.

The oak altar frontal at Llanmadoc church

Carved panel in Llanmadoc church

One of his notable achievements was to improve the frequency of celebrations of Holy Communion. When he was first appointed Holy Communion was celebrated six times a year at Llanmadoc and once a month at Cheriton. By 1877 he was recording in his visitation returns 70 celebrations a year for Llanmadoc and 30 for Cheriton. But the number of communicants did not noticeably increase. This was partly because both parishes had declining populations in the later years of his ministry but mainly because Davies believed in adequate preparation before communicating and was an advocate of non-communicating attendance at the Eucharist - a custom, which prevailed in many Anglo-Catholic churches into the 1940s and 1950s. Davies wrote a pamphlet advocating the practice: *A Few Words on Non-communicating Attendance* (Swansea 1879). Attendance figures are harder to come by but Davies was recording in 1900 an average attendance of 30 in the morning and 75 in the evening at Llanmadoc and 40 in the morning and 100 in the evening at Cheriton; not full houses but quite high figures for these small rural parishes.

Davies was a proficient carpenter and a talented wood-carver and used his skills to adorn his churches and raise funds for their restoration. The oak altar frontal at Llanmadoc is his work and it may have been carved in readiness for the church's re-opening ceremony in 1866. It has four panels each bearing a representation of one of the four evangelists. There is also in the church an elaborately carved panel, perhaps intended as a frontal for another altar but never used. But the finest examples of his skills are to be seen at Cheriton in the altar, altar rails, choir stalls and roof bosses. All this must have taken years of painstaking work. It is perhaps understandable that he never succeeded in producing work of this quality again.

To non-churchmen, Davies is perhaps best remembered as the author of the four-volumed *History of West Gower* that appeared between 1877 and 1894. (Sadly a fifth volume was never published, and the material lost.) The volumes are not really a history, rather a rich compendium or miscellany of essays, observations, documents, tales and legends. They will remain a rich quarry for the historian, antiquarian and student of Gower folklore and legend.

The Revd John David Davies died on Saturday, September 30th 1911, and was laid to rest in Cheriton churchyard on Wednesday 4th October 1911. He was a good classical scholar, priest, musician, woodcarver, archaeologist and linguist, but above all he was remembered "as a most loveable man." "Modest, kindly, all-accomplished, wise". "He was a man to all the country dear", and a hundred years later he is still revered in the villages he served.

Revd. J. D. Davies, rector, 1860-1911

Church Restoration at Llanmadoc and Cheriton

Deterioration in the church fabric through the passage of time and the effects of weather is a constantly recurring problem for parson and churchwardens. The usual method used to finance repairs before 1868 was to levy a church rate, but in small parishes like Llanmadoc and Cheriton this would not always provide a sum large enough to tackle major problems. It was easier to improvise, to mend and patch in a makeshift way and thereby try to avoid major extensive renovation. Even so the fabric was not neglected before the large-scale restorations of the later nineteenth century, as is sometimes suggested. Samuel Lewis in the *Topographical Dictionary of Wales* records that Llanmadoc was rebuilt in 1748 but we have no evidence of what this entailed. In 1821 when James Edwards was rector, Llanmadoc was considered "in good repair" and "receiving improvements by enlarging the windows", but we have to remember that what a parson or churchwarden would consider decent and acceptable in 1800 might not be so considered in 1860 or 1900. When Revd. J.D. Davies became rector in 1860 Llanmadoc church was, to use his own words to the diarist Kilvert, "meaner than the meanest hovel in the village". The replies of George Holland, churchwarden, to visitation queries put to him in the same year confirm this:

> "Very much out of repair. The roof is not secured. Doors very much out of repair. Pews in a most dilapidated condition. There are no new seats in the chancel. Earth allowed to lie against the walls and there are no spouts or drains to carry off the water. The bells are intact but the fittings in a wretched condition. The books are very much torn. There is a font but not in its proper position. There is a table (for Holy Communion) but no carpet or covering for it. There is a pulpit and reading desk but very much out of repair. There is a surplice in tolerably good condition. A church rate has been made this year, for the first time during several past years. Churchyard not sufficiently fenced. House belonging to minister in very bad repair. Minister has only just been presented to living and the house is now undergoing repairs."

We do not know how much the levy of a church rate raised but an interesting list of benefactors was printed in the Cambrian newspaper, which gives the contributions of each. The rector made the largest contribution. The next largest was made by the Lord Lieutenant who was, of course, C.R.M. Talbot, of Margam and Penrice. The total collected amounted to £585. 15s. 6d

The work of restoration began in 1865. Much of the south side of the nave, a portion of the upper part of the tower and the greater part of the east wall of the chancel had to be taken down and rebuilt. New windows were inserted in the east end of the chancel and the south side of the nave. When scraping off the whitewash and plaster on the north wall of the nave two round-headed, blocked-up apertures were uncovered. A new porch was built to replace an existing one, which had been constructed in such bad taste that the architect, John Prichard of Llandaff, felt compelled to remove it. The medieval water stoup, which the rector found in a garden in the village, was restored to the church.

The re-opening ceremony took place on 26th April 1866. It was performed with such ritual style that it caused a furore among low churchmen and nonconformists in Gower. Today it would not have called for particular comment but in the climate of religious opinion prevailing in the 1860s it was seen as a sinister threat to the Protestant establishment of evangelical Gower. A long and impassioned debate followed, conducted in the columns of the Cambrian newspaper. It lasted two whole months.

It took longer to raise the money for the restoration of Cheriton Church because it was larger and required more specialised treatment. With the abolition of church rates in 1868 Davies could no longer rely on this as a source of funding. He busied himself therefore with producing candlesticks, trays and book-cases for sale in church bazaars to swell the restoration fund. In 1873 his father died, and his mother in the following year. Davies must have put a considerable sum of his inheritance money into the restoration fund. By this time the church was in a sad state and action had to be taken to prevent fatal accidents. The minutes of the vestry meeting held on 16th July 1873 have been preserved in the faculty papers of the Church in Wales records at the National Library of Wales, Aberystwyth and give a vivid description of the condition of the fabric at this time:

"The parapet of the tower very shaky and much broken up, endangering the lives of the congregation, from the possibility of loose stones falling down at any moment, an accident of this kind already occurred, but happily when the church was empty. The said tower takes wet freely, the water percolating through the solid wall from top to bottom, drips from the arches on the inside, onto the floor of the church, and running along in a small stream, finds its way out at the door. The bell frame is much decayed, so as to endanger the fall of the bell. The several lofts of the tower are decayed, and in a very unsafe condition; the mortar is eaten out both externally and internally on the 4 sides, which will have to be pointed, and the loose stones fastened. The roofs of nave and chancel take wet where the slates abut against the walls. The architect proposes to put new roofs, altering the pitch and securing against wet with lead. A serious crack in the west gable of the nave threatens the destruction of that part, the repairing of which will probably involve the pulling down of some portion of the angle of the wall. The outer door of the porch is in a shattered condition. The roof of the porch is of a mean description irregularly put on, and open to the slates, the floor of earth, the mouldings of the inner doorway are mutilated and their beauty concealed by whitewash. The joists of the floor and planking have given way in many places and the bench ends rotted away. The whole of the interior of the church is whitewashed and streaked with green slime and other offensive stains. The alley is composed of concrete and broken up in some places. The chancel floor is principally of clay. The chancel will have to be re-arranged; a new communion table, chancel rail and other fittings will be required, regard being had to the decencies of religious worship. The want of a vestry has been greatly felt and it is proposed to erect one."

Altar at Cheriton church

Choir stall frontal at Cheriton church

Work now went ahead and in the course of it Davies found the pre-Reformation stone 'mensa' which formed the surface of the medieval altar. It had been used to form part of a step into the chancel. It was damaged, showing only three of the five consecration crosses on its surface. Davies had it carefully removed, "placing it", he wrote, "as nearly possible in its former position", and the present altar stands upon it. The restoration had cost £1,200. and the architect was John Prichard; the church was re-opened for services in 1875. The church was again renovated in 1934 and the church was re-opened for worship by the Bishop of Swansea and Brecon on 30th July, but no details of the work carried out appear to have survived.

Llanmadoc church, 1879

The Parsonages: Llanmadoc Rectory

The old rectory lay to the south of the church on or near the site of the present 'rectory'. As far as is known no drawing or photograph of it survives but it is described briefly in the parish terrier of 1755 as "a parsonage house containing 2 rooms upon the floor, with a dairy belonging to the same, a barn, stall and stable, containing abt 24 yards in length, a garden of abt 20 perches square, a rickyard containing abt 20 square perches."

During the rectorship of George Harris (1722-53) the dead body of George Thomas was found in the chimney of this house after he had attempted to burgle it. He was buried in unconsecrated ground within the ramparts of the hill fort on Llanmadoc Hill. The Revd J.D.Davies was in error in attributing this incident to the rectorship of Watkin Knight (1773-95). The correct facts are entered on the eighteenth century map of Llanmadoc in the West Glamorgan Record Office, for which see Hilary Thomas, *A Catalogue of Estate Maps* (Cardiff,1992), p98.

The rectory could not have been very large, for old people in Revd. J. D. Davies's day related that a former rector, Watkin Loughor Knight, was so fat that at his death in 1795 the coffin containing his body could not be brought down the stairs but had to be taken through the bedroom window and lowered to the ground by ropes. When the Revd. J.D. Davies was appointed rector, he had to stay at Glebe House until the widow of the former rector found a place to live. The churchwardens' visitation returns for 1860 describe the rectory as "in very bad repair". After repairs were completed Davies moved in. It is this old rectory which Francis Kilvert described in his diary in 1872: "the bare unfinished ugly barrack of a rectory...The house was thoroughly untidy and batchelor like and full of quaint odds and ends. The rigging of a boat stood in the hall, for the vicar is a great sailor and sails Carmarthen Bay in a boat built by himself". Davies decided to demolish this old rectory and he had the present one built on the site of the old in 1876.

The village story had always been that the Rector went to Switzerland, and on his return had enthusiastically set about building his new home. Part way through, however, matters had changed. The final bedroom doors on the first floor were evidently salvaged from other buildings, and though the stairs had been built to the second floor, the holes for flooring joists were never used, cheap ceiling joists being put in instead. The top storey was never completed. The Rector had obviously lost heart about finishing his home, and rumours went around that he must have been jilted by a potential Swiss bride.

In 2010 new evidence came to light. A letter from Revd. J. D. Davies to the Church Commissioners requested a loan from the Queen Anne's Bounty for £800, the amount that his architect, Benjamin Bucknall, expected the new rectory to cost. Davies intimated that he would pay anything above this amount himself. It is thought that the £800 figure is a gross underestimate of the finished cost, and the Rector would have been left with subsequent bills. Towards the end of his life the Rector wrote many letters to friends, explaining that he could not afford to publish his fifth volume on the History of West Gower, as he had run out of money, and it is likely that few realised the extent of his impoverished state.

Benjamin Bucknall had designed various buildings in Swansea, such as the old Swansea Grammar School on Mount Pleasant, the Seaman's Chapel in SA1, and the extension to the church of St David, besides other well known Churches and houses in both Wales and England. He is perhaps best known for his work on Woodchester Mansion. Benjamin Bucknall was a keen disciple of Viollet-le-Duc, the French scholar and restorer of medieval buildings. Between 1872 and 1876 Bucknall spent time commuting between Swansea and Lausanne in Switzerland, where Viollet-le-Duc was living, in order to translate his published works into English, sometimes taking friends with him. It is highly likely that Revd. J. D. Davies went as his guest. A photograph of Villa la Vedette, the home of Viollet-le-Duc, bears a remarkable resemblance to the side of Llanmadoc Rectory, whilst unused plans drawn up for the Leigh family at Woodchester mansion in 1874 no doubt influenced the style of the new Rectory.

Bucknall's plan for the Leigh family 1874

The Villa in Lausanne

Llanmadoc Rectory

Llanmadoc Rectory

In the 1870's Benjamin Bucknall also designed the new school on Llanmadoc hill for the Rector, who then spent a great deal of time and energy in raising money for this to be built too. It served the children of Llanmadoc, Cheriton and Llangennith well until 1935, and in 2010 was remembered fondly by several of its former pupils in a special "75 years on" Celebration.

When Davies entertained members of the Swansea Scientific Society in 1893, their report describes his workshop:

> "the framework of a modern house, not yet partitioned with separate chambers. Here the good rector has a remarkable collection of artistic ecclesiastical models, and a number of first class tools for the purpose of wood-shaping and wood-carving. The lathe, the drill, the fretsaw and the many other machines were attentively examined by the party. "

The workshop was on the site of a bungalow now called St Illtyd, a really central place within the village. The rectory was occupied by successive rectors until 1972, when the livings of Llanmadoc, Cheriton and Llanrhidian were grouped and the residence for the incumbent of the new benefice was at Llanrhidian. From 2005 Llanmadoc and Cheriton were regrouped with Llangennith, and the Vicarage is again in the latter village.

Glebe House, Cheriton

This is the oldest surviving domestic building in Gower and dates from the late thirteenth or early fourteenth century. It served as a rectory for the parish of Cheriton well into the eighteenth century. It consisted originally of a three-bay hall with a two-bay secondary unit, both open to the roof, joined to a cross-winged solar. The earliest description of the house is contained in the Cheriton parish terrier of 1720: "a parsonage house containing five rooms upon a floor. All lofted save ye hall belonging to ye same". The question immediately arises: how was a parsonage of this size built for a rector of a living valued at a mere £5. in 1291? And why was it built? It is tempting to think that the Knights Hospitallers at Slebech financed the building of Glebe House and perhaps the church too, and that the house was designed to act not only as a parsonage, but as a collecting centre for Slebech officials collecting dues from the order's extensive properties in the lordship of Gower. The quickest way from Slebech to these possessions in medieval times was by sea. Alternatively, the collectors might have made use, at low tide, of a passage on foot or horseback across the Burry estuary to Llanmadoc and Cheriton, as indeed John Wesley did when he was visiting his Methodist societies in Gower at the end of the eighteenth century.

The Revd. John Williams, junior, when he was rector of Cheriton, 1751-89, lived in the Great House, Cheriton (demolished in 1850). But he was once called in to lay a ghost at Glebe House. Williams was a scholar and a man of substance. He was a Fellow of King's College, Cambridge, held the rectory of Nicholaston as well as that of Cheriton, was prebendary of Brecon and chaplain to Lord Arbuthnot. The ghost at Glebe House was said to be of a lady who had once farmed Glebe and given false measure for the milk, butter and cheese she sold. Williams shut himself up in the "blue chamber" for two days and nights "the people of the house hearing him cracking his whip and talking Latin the whole time". It is also said that he got the mastery only by one word, and that the spirit was bound to make ropes of sand on Llanmadoc burrows and to remain there "till she done it".

The last rector to occupy Glebe House was John Williams, senior, who was rector from 1726 to 1751. From the 1840s on the licences issued to the Revd. William Lucas Collins dispensing him from residing in the parish throw some light on the condition of the house. In 1840 Glebe House was said to be "unfit for the residence of a clergyman, not having been so used in the memory of any person now living, and now tenanted by paupers." The licence for 1856 declared the house still unfit for the residence of the rector but said that the curate of Cheriton, Revd. James Shewen Swift, resided at the house of Philip Taylor. What the licence does not say is that Philip Taylor was the occupant of Glebe House. In 1860 the house was again declared unfit for residence "by reason of insufficiency of accommodation there being only one sitting room with earthen floor and the greater part of the house being unceiled, open to the rafters - apparently never at any period having been ceiled." This did not prevent curates of Cheriton living there as J.D. Davies did before his appointment to Llanmadoc. The house was ceiled, repaired and much improved in the later decades of the nineteenth century. In 1904 Mr. and Mrs. John Chalk, the tenants of Glebe House used it for the wedding reception of their daughter, Elizabeth. Revd. J.D.Davies declared this to be "the first wedding within living memory when singing and music were introduced into the ceremony. A hymn was sung and while the bride and groom signed the registers Mr. Ernest Helrne of Hillend played Mendelssohn's Wedding March".

Glebe House, Cheriton

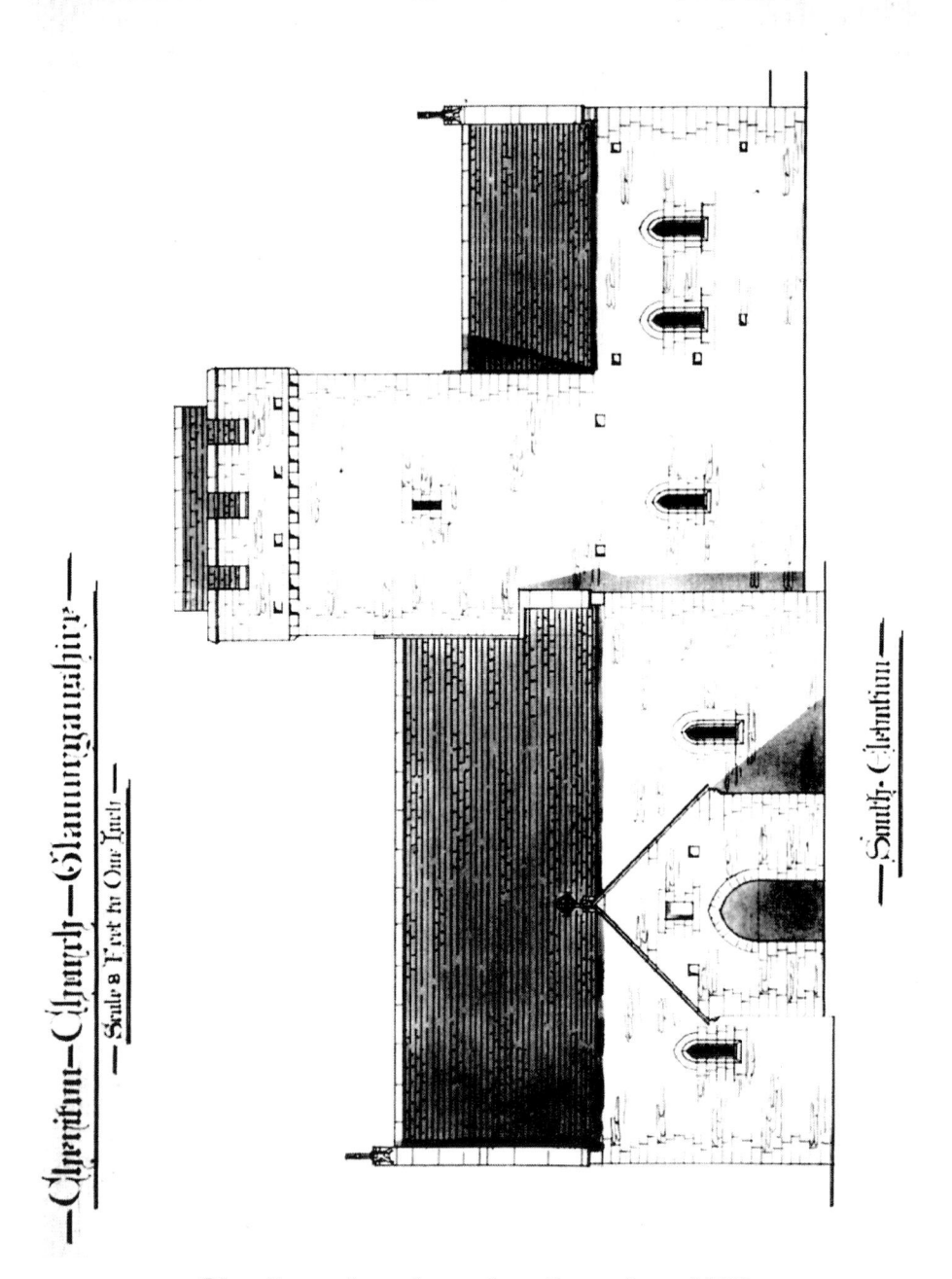

Cheriton church restoration plan, 1873

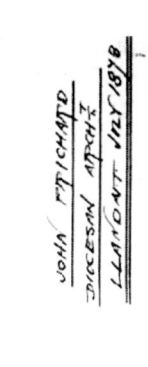

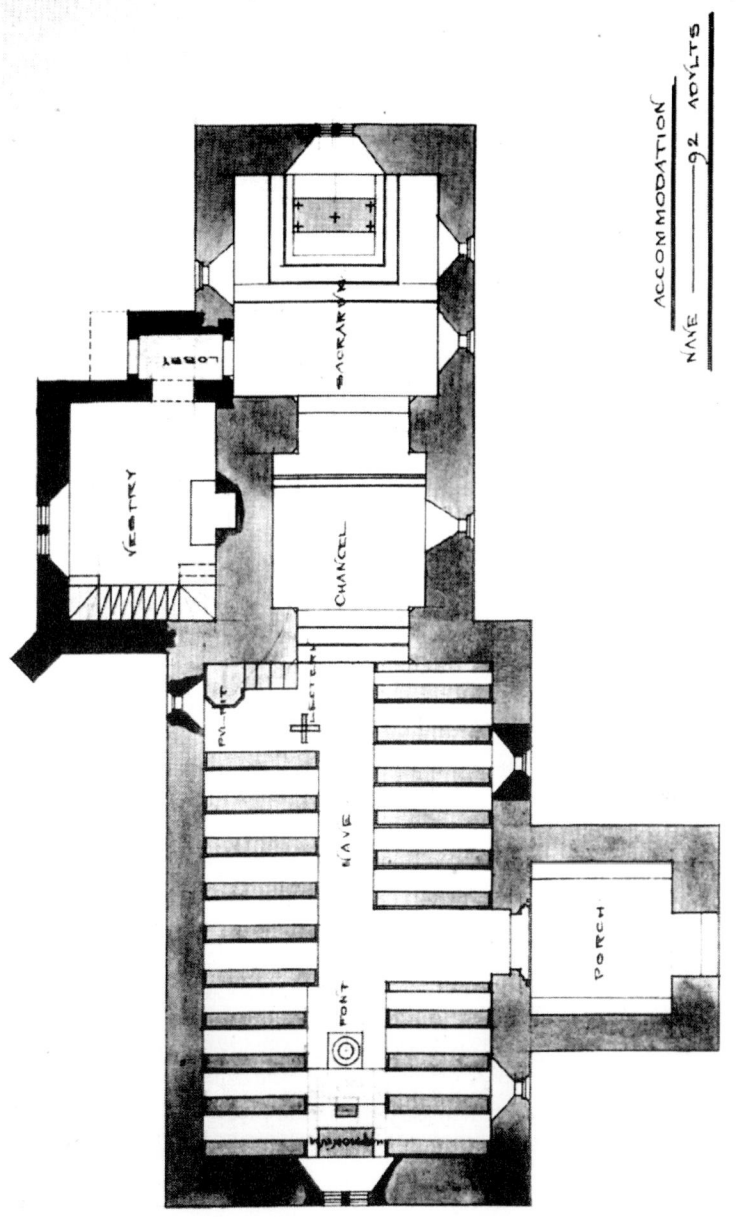

Cheriton church restoration plan, 1873

Change, Decay and the Decade of Evangelism

From the time when Iron Age farmers corralled their sheep and cattle and stored their grain behind the palisades of the hill fort on Llanmadoc Hill to the present day, agriculture has been the dominant feature of the economy of both parishes. It has preserved the main outlines of the rural landscape, of heath and common, of field and hedge-row from century to century. When J.D.Davies came to the parishes landowners of great wealth and influence had substantial holdings in the area. Sir Digby Thomas Aubrey held over 800 acres in Llanmadoc and C. R. M. Talbot, "the wealthiest commoner in England" had holdings of similar extent in Cheriton parish. Neither had houses in these parishes and their lands were leased out to local farmers.

(Following the sequestration of land from the Hospitallers, Queen Elizabeth 1st had finally sold the Manor of Llanmadoc to Anthony Mansel of Llantrithyd in 1559. His daughter Mary inherited it, and she had married Thomas Aubrey in 1586. Llanmadoc manorial lands then remained an Aubrey possession right through until their sale in 1924.)

There were a dozen or so farmers in each parish, some substantial freeholders like George Holland of Cwm Ivy who acted as unofficial resident squire. Others worked smaller holdings of only a few acres and combined farming with other occupations like quarrying and even teaching. The area was one of mixed farming; sheep and cattle were reared as well as grain grown. Both parishes had medium quality corn-growing land and produced wheat and barley which fed the five gristmills which survived in Davies's day from the seven which once worked along the Burry stream. The Census enumerator returns for 1851 record twenty-four agricultural labourers for Llanmadoc and twenty-two for Cheriton. Horses were shod and agricultural equipment serviced by one blacksmith in Llanmadoc and two in Cheriton. By 1891 there were four in Llanmadoc and one in Cheriton.

Both parishes had strong links with the sea mainly because of the lime and limestone industry. As early as 1639 a Penrice MS refers to quarries at Landimor "where tenants time out of mind have used to burn their lime for the composting of their lands". By the end of the eighteenth century there had developed a thriving industry in limestone and coal operated by small ship owners from Llanmadoc and Cheriton. Seamen in the two parishes were sufficiently numerous to attract the attention of the press gangs. An elderly labourer in Revd. J. D. Davies's day remembered that lightermen from these parishes used the cave in North Hill Tor as a hiding place from the press gangs during the French wars. "A good lookout was kept from the top of Llanmadoc Hill and as soon as the man of war's boat was seen coming from Llanelly, the intelligence was conveyed to the inhabitants, and all the young men, whether seafaring or otherwise, retired for safety to this cave."

In the 1830s and 1840s about thirty vessels, varying in burthen from twelve to twenty tons were engaged in carrying limestone from the Cwm Ivy and Tor Gro quarries to Cornwall and Devon and bringing culm and coal from Loughor and Llanelli to northwest Gower. Some Llanmadoc men owned much larger vessels. William Howell, mariner of Llanmadoc, owned "The Friends", a two-masted schooner of seventy-nine tons burthen between 1829 and 1846 and an eighth share in it was held by John Bevan, a Cheriton farmer. In 1838 William Evans of Llanmadoc had "The Gowerian" built. It was a two-masted schooner of sixty-seven tons burthen. The Census enumerator returns for 1841 record eight mariners, six master mariners and two pilots for Llanmadoc, while Cheriton in 1851 had five mariners and three master mariners. By Davies's day the coal and limestone trade was coming to an end. "Only two vessels remain," he wrote in1879,"bringing coal from Llanelly for the use of the inhabitants; the sinuous course of the pill for the last navigable mile, up to the rude and primitive wharf where the coals are landed, is marked by long rods, called 'pearches' stuck in the edges of the banks on either side." Davies during his long ministry also witnessed other changes. When he was appointed the population of Llanmadoc had peaked at two-hundred and sixty-nine and Cheriton at two hundred and eight-two. Thereafter the population fell, dropping to one hundred and fifty-four and one hundred and fifty-five respectively by 1891. Agricultural depression and the attraction of better paid jobs in coal mining and other industries were drawing many agricultural labourers to the Swansea valley and other parts of the South Wales coalfield.

Since Davies's death in 1911 the Aubrey and Talbot estates have been broken up and the age-old alliance of squire-landowner and parson has passed away. Farm mechanization has substantially reduced the numbers of those who work on the land but farms, though fewer, are now larger than they were in the mid-nineteenth century, and more compact. Rural industries and crafts were slow in dying. According to local memory the last farm lime kiln in Gower was at Hills Farm, Llanmadoc and it ceased operating in the 1930s. By then it was cheaper to purchase nationally-produced chemicals rather than to burn lime to fertilize the soil. The Stembridge grist mill, mentioned in the Cheriton parish terrier of 1720, ceased grinding about 1890. Isaac Tanner who left Whitemoor to take the mill, adapted the machinery to drive his weaving looms and Stembridge became a woollen factory. It continued to manufacture cloth until 1925. Cheriton mill, another woollen factory, was situated in the village. It was run in 1895 by Thomas Tanner and his son William. William Tanner continued weaving there until he died in 1932. The factory turned out blankets and cloths of all kinds, especially for suits, and William would carry them in a half-hundred weight pack on foot to Swansea. He would then take a train to Neath and sell his wares in Neath fair and walk home again.

The last blacksmith to operate in the two parishes was Mr. W. G. Watters who worked the forge opposite the Britannia Inn. It had been set up by his great grandfather early in the nineteenth century and it then made "jumpers", "spleets" and "briers" - quarrymen's tools - as well as providing a service for farmers. Mr. Watters had the roof of the forge re-thatched and its stonework repointed as recently as 1954 but it has since been abandoned and only ruined walls now remain. Four public houses, the Britannia, Farmer's Arms, Old Ship and Mariners once slaked the thirst of the mixed population of farmers, quarrymen, weavers and seamen. Today only the Britannia survives of the village pubs. Danes Dyke, quite near the village, took over the licence of the Farmer's Arms in the late 1960s and operated as a licensed restaurant, but is now in private hands.

Two closely-related new developments have halted, if not reversed, the trend of falling population: improved transport and tourism. In the last decades of the Revd. J. D. Davies's ministry Llanmadoc and Cheriton were still remote and isolated villages. Horse buses ran three times a week and carried live-stock, dairy produce, farm and kitchen utensils as well as passengers to and from Swansea, a journey that could take three hours or more each way. Brakes or wagonettes owned by the more affluent would take roughly the same time. After 1909 motor buses began operating and gradually provided a faster, more reliable and comfortable ride between Swansea and the villages of West Gower. But the most significant developments have been the rapid growth of private car ownership since the 1950s and the improvement of road surfaces. The journey time between Swansea and Llanmadoc has now been reduced to not much over thirty minutes outside peak periods. This transport revolution has made Llanmadoc and Cheriton desirable places in which to live, not only for the retired but for business and professional people who work in Swansea and even farther afield. It has also enabled Llanmadoc to develop as a tourist centre with camping and caravanning facilities which attract hundreds of people to the area in the summer months. Tourism has become an important, if seasonal, part of the local economy.

In 1920 the Church of England in Wales was disestablished by act of Parliament. The Church in Wales was thereby separated from the English state and became a distinct province of the Anglican communion with its own archbishop and machinery of government. Disestablishment, pushed forward by radical politicians, Liberals and nonconformists, had been dreaded by most churchmen. They feared the Church would suffer financial bankruptcy and that its pastoral mission would be seriously impeded by continuing nonconformist expansion. Neither of these fears were eventually justified. Another organizational change affected Gower more directly. The churches in the Welsh commote of Gower had in 1133 been adjudged by an ecclesiastical court to belong to the diocese of St. David's and their parishes were formed into a deanery which corresponded in area with the newly-formed lordship of Gower. The Gower deanery and its later nineteenth century sub-divisions continued to belong to the large, sprawling diocese of St. David's until 1923 when the diocese of Swansea and Brecon was created and Gower became one of its new archdeaconries. As we have seen earlier, the parishes of Llanmadoc and Cheriton were formed into a consolidated living by an act of the Privy Council in 1868. In 1927 an archdiaconal commission of enquiry recommended that both parishes should be linked with Llangennith, that the incumbent should reside at Llanmadoc and the curate at Llangennith. This recommendation was never implemented. But in 1972 Llanmadoc and Cheriton were linked with Llanrhidian, and the new incumbent, Revd. W. H. Bateman, who was vicar of Llanrhidian, became the first incumbent of the new grouping, and continued to reside in the vicarage at Llanrhidian. Since 2005 Llanmadoc and Cheriton have been linked with Llangennith, with the incumbent residing at Llangennith.

Accompanying these organizational re-arrangements and partly prompting them, there have been changes of a more fundamental and disturbing kind. There has been in the present century throughout Western Europe a marked decline in the number of people attending church and chapel. There has been too a marked fall in the number of vocations to the Christian ministry.

When the diocese of Swansea and Brecon was created in 1923, it was served by one hundred and eighty three clergy. By 1973 the number had dropped to one hundred and thirty three and it now stands at one hundred and eighteen. There are various reasons for this retreat from organized religion. In Victorian times many had been disturbed by the new discoveries of geology and evolutionary zoology which were perceived to be undermining the literal truth and accuracy of events in scripture, and many have still not been able to reconcile the new world picture created by science with religious belief. But more potent forces have also been at work. The rising tide of affluence after the 1950s, the lure of television and organized sport, the growth of car ownership and the lavish provision of leisure facilities have taken a heavy toll on church attendance. The church in town and village is no longer the cultural and recreational centre it once was. It has virtually lost its role in education to the state schools and many of its other roles to local and central government agencies. It is against this background of social change and declining church membership that the Lambeth Conference in 1988 proclaimed the 1990s as a Decade of Evangelism. "Evangelism", said Archbishop Noakes in 1990, "is concerned with communication...The challenge of the Church in the nineties is to become the heart of the community, reaching out beyond itself to touch and transform those who are outside the circle of church goers". It is to be hoped that the material restoration of Cheriton church, started in 1993, will be locally one symbolic marker on the journey towards the spiritual recovery of the Christian church in west Gower for which we all pray.

June 1993.

June 2011.

Appendices
LIST OF INCUMBENTS - Rectors of Llanmadoc

John Herry	Occurs 1400, resigned 1408
Richard Seynt alias Lintcumbe	Instituted 1408
Master Fawie	Occurs 1488
Maurice ap David	1488-91
John David or Davy	Occurs 1491 and 1535
Nicholas Lewis	1542-45
Nicholas Batcock	1545-54
Thomas Davys	1554-86
Daniel Battcock	1586-1613
Hugh Powell	1613-14
William Williams	1614-17
William Awbrey	1617-19
Hugh Vaughan	1619-40
William Edwards	1640-
George Parry	Occurs 1649, ejected c.1650-51, re-instated 1661 and rector until his death in 1678
John Williams	1678-1701
Peter Meantis	1701-22
George Harris	1722-53
Richard Price	1753-72
Watkin Loughor Knight	1772-95
Samuel Davies	1795-97
Samuel Davies	1797-1810
Hector Bowen	1810-21
James Edwards	1821-33
Prosser Pearce	1835-60
John David Davies	1860-68 Hereafter see under Llanmadoc with Cheriton

Rectors of Cheriton

William Gower	Occurs 1419
David Jones	Occurs 1535
Henry Holland	1565-
Nicholas Harry	Occurs 1583
Matthew Bennett	1610-
George Parry	Occurs 1649, ejected, then re-instated 1661 and rector until his death in 1678
John Williams	1678-1701
William Williams	1701
William Hopkins	1701-26
John Williams senior	1726-51
John Williams junior	1751-87
Benjamin Jones	1788-1840
William Lucas Collins	1840-67

Rectors of Llanmadoc with Cheriton

John David Davies	1868-1911
Edwin David Perrott Bush	1912-22
Henry John Evans	1922-32
Harold Victor Williams	1932-45
Il. Llewelyn Jones	1945-54
Meredydd Howells	1954-58
John Thomas Hughes Evans	1958-71

Rectors of Llanrhidian with Llanmadoc and Cheriton

William Henry Bateman	1972-82
David Wayne Evans Brinson	1982-91
Joseph William Griffin	1991-99
John Eldon Phillips	1999-2005

Rectors of Llanmadoc, Cheriton and Llangennith

Peter J. Williams	2005 -

THE CHURCH BELLS
Llanmadoc

A single bell in the west tower inscribed:

> (Lion) PHILLIPP HARIS EVAN JENKIN
>
> G.P. R (bell) A C.P.(Lion) 1675 Diameter 26½"
>
> W.H. R.H. P.H. E.P. G.L. C.P. S.P. G.H.

Philip Harris and Evan Jenkin were the churchwardens. G.P. is George Parry, the rector; R.A. the bell founder cannot be identified. The remaining initials are of the parishioners who subscribed to the founding of the bell. There was another bell according to Revd. J.D. Davies, but having cracked, it was removed and later either stolen or surreptitiously sold.

Cheriton

A single bell in the central tower inscribed:

> **W (bell) E. 1736 Diameter 20½"**

The bell was cast by William Evans of the Chepstow bell foundry who cast bells between 1710 and 1767.

THE CHURCH PLATE (no longer kept in church)
Llanmadoc

1. Silver Elizabethan chalice and patent cover bearing the hall marks of 1573 with maker's mark, a windmill, for Robert Knight, a London goldsmith. Inscribed on lip of bowl:
   > *POCULUM* ECCLESIAE . DE LANMAD(OK)
2. Victorian silver chalice (hall-marked 1866) and paten (hall- marked 1857) with maker's mark IK. Presented to the church by Revd. Richard Meux Benson in 1866.

Cheriton

1. Silver chalice of reign of Charles I. bearing the hall-mark of 1640, with maker's mark indistinct but possibly RC in a shaped shield. Close to the lip of the bowl is inscribed:
   > **"CHERITON PARISH"**
   > **1730**
   There is no paten cover.
2. Silver Victorian chalice and paten of parcel-gilt, bearing the hall marks of 1874 with maker's mark SS. Of modern medieval pattern having the sacred monogram on one of the six panels of the base. Paten engraved in centre with the sacred monogram.
3. Silver Victorian paten with foot, hall marked 1859 with illegible maker's mark, the centre being ornamented with the sacred monogram and cross.

THE STAINED GLASS

Llanmadoc

East window of two lights with quatrefoil. A memorial window for Francis and Jane Anne Bevan of Glebe Farm, Llanmadoc, erected by their three grandchildren. Made by Celtic Studios, Swansea, 1950. In left-hand light, a farmer and his wife in medieval dress bringing the fruits of their labour to give to the Christ figure in right-hand light. In the quatrefoil above is a harvest field with golden sheaves, a mown field and a cottage.

Cheriton

East window of two lights in memory of Revd. J.T.H. Evans, rector 1958-71 and his son Michael. Made by Celtic Studios, Swansea and erected 1973. The Revd. J.T.H. Evans played for the Llanelli Rugby Club in the 1930s and was a trialist for Wales. The left-hand window features the crown, orb and sceptre of Christ the King, a white pelican piercing its breast to feed its young with its blood, a symbol of Christ's sacrifice on the cross, and the eucharistic chalice. The right-hand light features a dove representing the Holy Spirit, a golden phoenix rising from the flames, representing the Resurrection and at the base the Chi Rho sign with alpha and omega on either side.

West window of two lights with quatrefoil above in memory of Frederica Ebeling and grandson Colin Ross. Made by Celtic Studios, Swansea in mid-1970s. In left-hand light a tree of life rising against a Celtic cross; in the right-hand one, a dove of peace, bearing a cross shining down on a font of blue water. The theme in letters above: HOLY BAPTISM. In the quatrefoil a Paschal lamb bearing the flag of St. George.

FONTS

Llanmadoc

A square shaped font probably of twelfth-century date set on a modern base.

Cheriton

1. A tub-shaped Norman style font in chancel. Half of the bowl broken off. It may have come from an earlier church.
2. A modern font of freestone, octagonal in shape and lined with lead.

MEMORIALS
Llanmadoc

In addition to the important pre-Norman stones which have already been dealt with, there is a brass memorial plaque on the north wall of the chancel to Revd. J.D. Davies, rector 1860-1911, erected by his parishioners. On the south wall of the chancel is a memorial tablet to Revd. W.L. Knight, rector 1772-95.

A Hymn Board, donated by W. A. Bosley, commemorating the consecration of the new burial ground on August 26th 1930.

Cheriton

On either side of the altar are two marble memorials set into the floor. The one on the south side is a memorial with epitaph to Revd. John Williams, M.A., prebendary of Brecon and rector of Cheriton who died 31st January 1787 and to his wife, Ann who died in 1806. The memorial on the north side is to Barbara Williams, died 1831 and Elizabeth Williams, died 1836, both daughters of Revd. John Williams.

Below the west window is a stone tablet memorial set into the wall to George, son of William Tuck who died 1739, and others.

A brass memorial to men of Llanmadoc and Cheriton who fell in World War I is fixed above the pulpit. A memorial to those who gave their lives in World War II is of Welsh slate and placed above the organ.

SOURCES
Manuscript

ABERYSTWYTH. National Library of Wales.

MS 1626C,1627C. Clerical Institutions Wales ending 1840.
Church in Wales Records. SD/F 109. Faculty for restoration of Cheriton church.
                SD/NR 161-7 Licences for non-residence (Cheriton)
                SD/QA 61-120 (1755-1906). Visitation questions and answers, clergy and churchwardens.

SWANSEA. University College Library.
    Microfilm copies of Census enumerator returns for Llanmadoc and Cheriton from originals in Public Record Office.

SWANSEA. West Glamorgan Record Office.
    Cheriton parish: tithe map and schedule. 1846
    Llanmadoc parish: tithe map and schedule. 1845.

PRINTED

BARKER, T.W.	*Particulars relating to endowments etc. of Livings. Vol 1* Archdeaconry of Carmarthen (Carmarthen 1907)
BROADY, M.	Unpublished notes on stained glass in Gower churches.
BUCKNALL, Stephen	"Benjamin Joseph Bucknall, disciple of Viollet-Le-Duc, and his brothers Robert and Alfred. *Minerva II* (1994), 8 – 14
BUCKNALL, Stephen A.	*Benjamin Bucknall 1833 – 1895: a brief biography* (Woodchester, 1989)
BUTLER, L.A.S.	'Medieval ecclesiastical architecture in Glamorgan and Gower', *Glamorgan County History,* III (1971), 379-415.
CHURCH IN WALES,	*Diocese of Swansea and Brecon, Commission of enquiry in the Archdeaconry of Gower* (Swansea 1927).
COLLINS, M.H. & AIRD, E.C.	*The Collins Family* (2 vols. Ardmore, Pennsylvania, 1976-7).

COLLINS GUIDE TO PARISH CHURCHES IN ENGLAND AND WALES,
                ed. J. Betjeman(London,1980).

CRAIG, R.	'Notes on the shipping of the south Burry', *Gower* IX (1956), 43-7.
DAVIES, E.T., WILLIAMS, G. & ROBERTS, G.	'Religion and education in Glamorgan, 1660-c.1775', *Glamorgan County History,* IV (1974), 431-533.
DAVIES, J.D.	*A History of West Gower* (4 vols Swansea 1877-94).

DICTIONARY OF WELSH BIOGRAPHY DOWN TO 1940 (London, 1959).

THE EPISCOPAL REGISTERS OF ST. DAVID'S, 1397-1518, ed. R. F. Isaacson (3 vols.London,1917-20).

EVANS, J. T. *The church plate of Gowerland* (Stow-on-the Wold1921).

GOWER CHURCH MAGAZINE, 1900-

JONES, I.G. & WILLIAMS, D. eds. *The religious census of 1851: a calendar of returns for Wales Vol.1 South Wales* (Cardiff 1976)

KNIGHT J.K. 'Glamorgan A.D. 400-1100: archaeology and history', *Glamorgan County History,* II (1984), 315-64.

KNIGHT J.K. 'Sources for the early history of Morgannwg', *Glamorgan County History II,* (1984), 365-455.

LEWIS S. *A topographical dictionary of Wales, Vol.11* (3rd ed. London, 1843).

LLOYD, J.D.K. 'The historian of West Gower', *Gower VI* (1953) 7-9.

LUCAS, R.L.T. *A Gower family: the Lucases of Stouthall and Rhosili rectory* (Lewes,1986).

LUCAS,R.L.T. 'Parson Davies', *Gower* XXVIII (1977), 5-15.

LUCAS R.L.T. 'Llanmadoc and the Scarlet Woman', *Gower,* XXXIII (1982), 75-79.

NASH-WILLIAMS, V.E. *The Early Christian Monuments of Wales* (Cardiff, 1950).

ORRIN, G.K. 'The church bells of Gower', *Gower,* XXXIX (1988), 52-62.

ORRIN, G.R. *The Gower Churches* (Swansea, 1979).

REES, W. *A History of the Order of St. John of Jerusalem in Wales and on the Welsh Border* (Cardiff, 1947).

REES, W. 'The Templar Manor of Llanmadoc', *Bulletin of the Board of Celtic Studies,* XIII (1950), 144-5.

ROBINSON, W.R.B. 'The Church in Gower before the Reformation' *Morgannwg,* XIII (1968), 5-36.

ROYAL COMMISSION ON ANCIENT AND HISTORICAL MONUMENTS IN WALES, *Glamorgan: the Early Castles from the Norman Conquest to 1217* (Cardiff, 1992.).

ROYAL COMMISSION ON ANCIENT & HISTORICAL MONUMENTS IN WALES,
*An Inventory of the Ancient Monuments in Glamorgan,
Vol.1. Pre-Norman* (Cardiff, 1976).

ROYAL COMMISSION ON ANCIENT & HISTORICAL MONUMENTS IN WALES,
An Inventory of the Ancient Monuments in Glamorgan Vol. Ill Medieval secular monuments, Part II:Non-defensive' (Cardiff, 1982).

SODDEN, R.W. *Guide to Welsh Parish Churches* (Llandysul 1984).

SWANSEA AND GLAMORGAN CALENDAR.
Compiled and annotated by W.C. Rogers, (3 Vols. Swansea 1941-6).

TAYLOR, B.S.   'The water mills of Gower: an historical perspective', *Gower*, XLII (1991), 6-23.

TOFT, L.A.   'The Gower lime burning industry, 1800-1960', *Gower*, XXXIX (1988), 64-74.

TOFT, L.A.   'Lime burning on the Gower peninsula's limestone belt'. *Industrial Archaeology Review,* XI (1988), 75-85.

TUCKER, H.M.   *Gower Gleanings* (Swansea, 1951).

TUCKER, H.M.   *My Gower* (Neath, 1957).

TUCKER H,M,   'There's no sign of decline in the old business at Llanmadoc (the Llanmadoc smithy)', *South Wales Evening Post.* 11th June 1954.

Acknowledgements

Acknowledgement is made to Mr Royston Kneath for the colour photographs used on the cover and to Mr Andy Freem for the four photographs on pp.15 and 20.

The line drawing of the Advectus stone and the print of Llanmadoc church on pp.1 and 21 are from J.D.Davies, *History of West Gower, vol.II* and the views on pp.9 and 11 are from *Eight views of churches and castles in South Wales* (Tenby, 1850)

The photograph of Revd. J.D.Davies on p.17 is reproduced by kind permission of Peter and Sally Lyne.

The cutaway drawing of Glebe House on p.35 is Crown copyright and reproduced by permission of the Royal commission on Ancient and Historical Monuments of Wales.

The Brecon Diocesan Office have kindly provided the current figures for diocesan clergy on page 31.

Benjamin Bucknall's drawing on page 23 has been reproduced by permission of the Woodchester Mansion Trust.

Mike and Brenda Bristow are thanked for preparing the manuscript for publication for the first edition.

Thanks are due to the Gower Society for their help and support with this edition.

I owe a special debt of gratitude to Sally Lyne and Neil Wilson, who have been very much involved at all stages in the production of this 2011 edition.

"The School on the hill" …..

….. Children at Cheriton and Llanmadoc School

A view from the hill towards Llanmadoc Church

A view from the hill towards Cheriton Church